Weekend Mischief

Weekend Mischief

Poems by Rob Jackson

Illustrations by Mark Beech

Honesdale, Pennsylvania

Text copyright © 2010 by Rob Jackson
Illustrations copyright © 2010 by Mark Beech
All rights reserved

Wordsong
An Imprint of Boyds Mills Press, Inc.
815 Church Street
Honesdale, Pennsylvania 18431
Printed in China

First edition
The text of this book is set in 14-point Minion.
The illustrations are done in watercolor and
pen and ink.

10 9 8 7 6 5 4 3 2 1

Library of Congress Cataloging-in-Publication Data

Jackson, Robert Bradley.
  Weekend mischief / Rob Jackson ; illustrated by Mark Beech. —
1st ed.
     p. cm.
   ISBN 978-1-59078-494-5 (hardcover : alk. paper)
  1. Boys—Juvenile poetry. 2. Children's poetry, American. I.
Beech, Mark. II. Title.
   PS3610.A3548W44 2009
   811'.6—dc22
                                                 2009019916

For Will, who still crosses his eyes
—R.J.

To my niece, Evie
—M.B.

Contents

The Grumpus 8
Early Crime 9
Not Again 10
The Fair... 12
Crosseyed... 13
Time Change 14
Super Cuts 15
Road Trip... 16
Tell Me 18
Homework.. 19
Workdays... 20
Bored 21
The Law 22
Campfire.. 23
Sunflower Seeds 24
Winter Clothes 25
Haiku Hello 26
Commander in Chief....................................... 28
Bedtime... 30
Rising 31

The Grumpus

Saturday morning I'm lying in bed
Happy, no worries or cares
When into my head bumps a sound that I dread—
A bellowing beast clumps upstairs

"Get out of bed! There's work to be done!"
Suddenly in stomps the Grumpus
My brother and I try to hide in our sheets
We know if he finds us, he'll thump us

If thumps haven't worked, he'll make a cold shower
Rain on us, buckets not trickles
When no water's left, he says, "Up, lazy bums!"
Then wriggles his fingers and tickles

Resist? Not a chance, we fall out of bed
Complaining but not really mad
We don't mind a Grumpus who smiles when he bites
In case you don't know, he's our dad

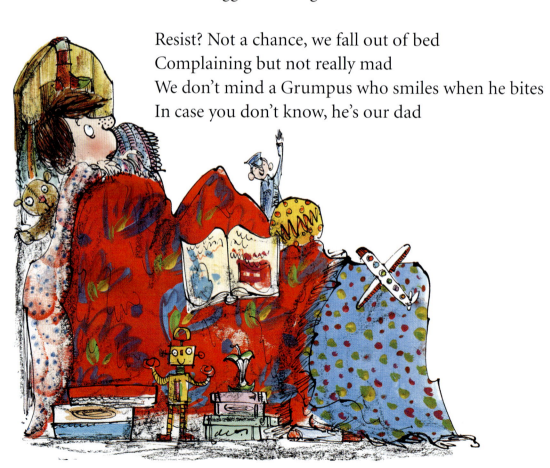

Early Crime

Warm biscuits
One crisp autumn morning
Cool on the counter
We strike without warning
First there are thirty
Then twenty
Then ten
We swallow the evidence
Vanish again

Not Again

Cut the grass
It grows again
Rake the leaves
It blows again
Shovel snow
It snows again
Stop a leak
It flows again

Tape a page
It rips again
Scold a pup
It nips again
Float your boat
It tips again
Wipe your nose
It drips again

Fix a toy
It breaks again
Nurse a bruise
It aches again
Dry the dog
It shakes again
Clean some mud
It cakes again

I pray the day is coming when
I never hear that word *again*

The Fair

Tickets and teddy bears, fooling with friends
Ice cream that drips on my shoes
Ring toss and rodeo, World's fattest man!
Clowns with balloons and kazoos

Too short to ride on the Death Ray before
This year at last I grew up
We zoom and we twirl, we dive and we whirl
Oh nice, some kid just threw up

Prowling the midway, I'm looking for food—
Hot dogs and ketchup that squirts
Funnel cakes, Snickers bars, anything fried
Suddenly my stomach hurts

Crawl to the car where I groan on the seat
"Don't let me barf, Mom, amen."
The end of my best-ever day at the fair
Tomorrow, let's do it again

Crosseyed

Mom said never cross your eyes
Or else you'll get a bad surprise
I laughed, but now I'm out of luck
Because my eyes won't come unstuck

Time Change

Yesterday I hid inside
And caught my parents when they tried
To set the clock two hours ahead
And trick me into early bed

So tonight I'll sneak-attack
And set the clock four hours back
They'll never know in all our fun
That bedtime's really half past one

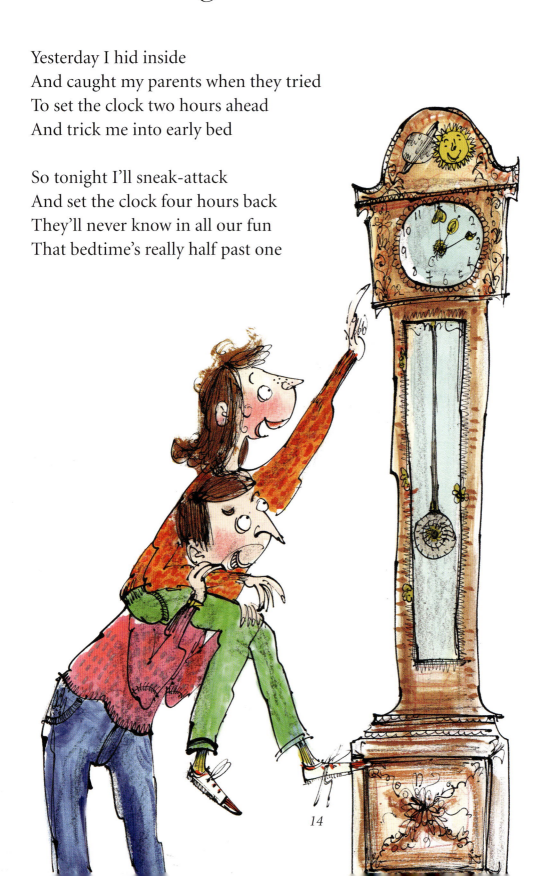

Super Cuts

She dragged me inside
Where I looked in the eye
Of a dark, evil lord
I was too young to die

He slashed with his sword
Then he hacked at my forehead
I looked for some armor,
A weapon, a warhead

That demon of darkness
Attacked me again
I fought for my life
Kicked him hard in the shin

I saw his eyes water
And heard the beast bellow
He sliced with his clippers
I wriggled like Jell-O

"Sit Still!" screamed my mom.
"Let him finish your hair."

I'm trapped at the barbershop
Life isn't fair

Road Trip

Pack my suitcase, stuff the car
Our weekend trip begins today
We're heading off to someplace far
With lots to see along the way

We leave the interstate behind
Ignore McDonald's, Colonel Sanders
Find some smaller roads that wind
A slower trail that still meanders

We buy some ice-cold lemonade,
Some roadside sweets and watermelon
Find sisters selling treats they made
Eat cookies "Baked by Sal and Helen"

We pass an old man on a bike
Who grins and waves at all the cars
He pats a dog I really like
It's riding on the handlebars

Power poles for miles on miles
With shoes thrown on the power line
I see them hanging there and smile
Because I know the shoes aren't mine

At last a friendly home's in sight
We count the stars no more
I slam the car door in delight
And run to my grandma's door

Tell Me

Who made the rule that dessert is served last?
That math class goes slowly and recess goes fast?
That Christmas must come at the *end* of the year?
That small kids go first, and big kids to the rear?

Why is the prize in the cereal pack
Never as good as the picture on back?
And how come it rains on the weekend but then
Gets sunny on Monday when school starts again?

I've asked politely, I've even tried yelling
Neither one helps, because no one is telling

Homework

It's good to do your own work
But I don't like alone work
I called some friends for their work
They told me that's not fair work

I found twin sister's schoolwork
She yelled, "NO WAY! Now you'll work.
You're not supposed to steal work.
Get lost and do some real work."

So here I am with no work
With nothing-more-to-show work
For hours I've tried to spy work
I guess I'll try out my work

Workdays

Saturday means a workday ahead
I keep myself busy from breakfast to bed
Seeing how far paper airplanes will glide
And how long a cucumber spins on its side
I sprawl on the sofa while tossing a pillow
Lie down in the grass counting leaves on a willow
Hammer a box full of nails in a board
Practice some strokes with my best wooden sword
Spin in my dad's twirly chair till I'm dizzy
When he says, "Do homework!"
I answer, "I'm busy!"

Bored

I wish I were on board a ship,
The captain of a pirate crew

Or revving up an outboard engine,
Racing past a slow canoe

Or chairman of the board of Toys,
A world of games to play for free

Instead I'm bored
Because there's
Nothing fun
To do.
Poor
Me

The Law

I hate it at home or at school
When I'm forced to follow each rule
Like "Love one another,"
"Be kind to your brother."
They can't make me do it. It's cruel.

Campfire

My dragon
Is fierce enough
To brag on

Gray smoke
Pours out his ears
Enough to gag on

He shoots out flames
Of reds and yellows
I use his fire
To cook marshmallows

And my friend the unicorn
Roasts the marshmallows on its horn
The whole bag on

Sunflower Seeds

Mountains and mountains of sunflower seeds
It really isn't my fault
I love to munch the plain ones
And the ones sprinkled with salt

For years I smuggled them into my room
Stuffed in my pockets and pants
Then I came up with the brilliant idea
Of filling my room full with plants

I turn on the bath, and let water run
Into my bedroom each night
I leave on the overhead lights all the time
To keep my plants happy and bright

Now my room's so full of sunflower stalks
Sprouting from seeds that I spit
That I keep the lawn mower running
To cut out a place I can sit

My bedroom's a sunflower garden
A field of flowery smells
I only leave now when I need to go dump
The wheelbarrow loaded with shells

Winter Clothes

I didn't want to go outside
With snow and ice around
"OK," I said, "I'll get my clothes."
And this is what I found

I first put on my underwear
A pair of socks and pants
What's in there? Whoa! A bear, a hare
A furry fox and ants

Inside the sleeve of my new shirt
And sleeping in my sweater
I found a soggy sea squirt
And an Irish setter

Next I grabbed a winter hat
A woolen scarf, and gloves
But hiding there, a cloud of bats
And nesting turtledoves

Last of all, inside my coat
And floating in my shoes
A walrus and a billy goat
Were waiting for some gnus

With friends like these I stayed inside
And opened up a zoo

It's true

Haiku Hello

Frost on a window
My fingers leave a message
For my brother—

Commander in Chief

Read THIS! mom and dad
My first White House letter
The President says
I can do your job better

And as your new Boss
I can never be wrong
I'm no longer Short Stuff
Just call me King Kong

I'm Lincoln and Washington
Superman, Caesar
Salad? No way,
Pizza fresh from the freezer

I'll stay up all night
With my friends, drinking coffee
Play soccer inside
Eating ice cream and toffee

We'll zoom through the halls
Riding round on our bicycles
Shut off the heat
And grow living-room icicles

Turn on the hose
Grab my goldfish and carry them
Into my new flooded
Bedroom aquarium

Splashing my pictures
Around big and glossy
I'm Chief of the Chiefs,
Sir, yes SIR, the Big Bossy

"OH RIGHT," said my parents,
"Your letter's a phony.
For lunch you get
Broccoli, squash, no baloney."

Bedtime

All day long I zip around
Inside, outside, fast as light
But BEDTIME brings the word I dread
As time slows to a crawl each night

Not YET! There's homework I forgot
And clothes to fold before time passes
I'll never make it up the stairs
My muscles have become molasses

Next I need the *right* pajamas
Can't forget to brush my teeth
Ten minutes for the ones on top
And ten more for the ones beneath

Finally, I think I'm ready
But my parents went to bed
I wonder why they couldn't wait
To say good-night to me instead

So quiet as a mouse I sneak
My flashlight and my radio
In bed with me to read a book,
Hear baseball with the sound down low

Rising

I dreamed that I was standing by
A river flowing dark and deep
And hooked a fish that swam below—
A prize I fought to catch and keep
My rod bent double as it pulled
I reeled it in with all my strength
It swam away, I hauled it back
Then finally I saw its length—
A fish beyond my wildest dreams
I reached to lift it from the pool
But my alarm clock pulled me up
From deep in sleep I woke for school

Rob Jackson is a writer and scientist at Duke University. He studies plants and animals all over the world. At home, he watches his three sons cause mischief along with the family's goats, pheasants, chickens, and dog.

Mark Beech, who lives in London, England, has illustrated a number of books for children, including *Trolls, Go Home!* and other books in the Troll Trouble series by Alan MacDonald.